Texas

Second Edition

Includes Inland, Coastal, and Offshore Sites

**Barbara Dunn and Janet R. Edwards
Photographs by Stephan Myers**

 Pisces Books®
A division of Gulf Publishing Company
Houston, Texas

All photographs by Stephan Myers, except where noted

Copyright © 1990, 1997 by Gulf Publishing Company, Houston, Texas. All rights reserved. This book, or parts thereof, may not be reproduced in any form without permission of the publisher.

Pisces Books®

A division of Gulf Publishing Company
P.O. Box 2608
Houston, Texas 77252-2608

Pisces Books is a registered trademark of Gulf Publishing Company.

Printed in Hong Kong

10   9   8   7   6   5   4   3   2   1

Library of Congress Cataloging-in-Publication Data

Dunn, Barbara,
    Diving and snorkeling guide to Texas : includes inland, coastal, and offshore sites / Barbara Dunn and Janet R. Edwards. — 2nd ed.
        p.   cm.
    ISBN 1-55992-091-2
    1. Deep diving—Texas—Guidebooks.   2. Skin diving—Texas—Guidebooks.   3. Texas—Guidebooks.   I. Edwards, Janet R.   II. Title.
GV840.S78D85   1996
797.2′3′09764—dc20   96-8596
                                                                CIP

Table of Contents

Marine organisms encrust every square inch of the underwater structures of a rig. A diver can see large barnacles, hydroid, bryzoans, many colorful fish and interesting invertebrates.

Introduction

When it comes to land and resources, there's just no place like Texas. The nearly 270,000 square miles that our state claims is so vast that it even encompasses the four major geographical areas found on the North American continent. We have our own Great Plains in north central Texas, Great Western High Plains in the Panhandle, Rocky Mountains in West Texas, and Gulf Coastal Plains along the coast. Within a day's drive, you can travel from endless sandy beaches on the coast to mile-high elevations, in the Guadalupe Mountains, from the moist, heavy air of East Texas' piney woods to the parched desolation of the Panhandle.

There is one aspect about the land that is constant nearly all over the state and into the Gulf of Mexico. Beneath all this diversity, the immense forces of the earth have formed faults hundreds of miles long. Some of these faults have trapped oil, while others have opened the surface to pulsing veins of ground water. The results of these changes can be seen in the crystalline, spring-fed lakes and rivers across the state. Offshore, similar forces changed the floor of the Gulf of Mexico, lifting isolated areas closer to the water surface and enabling tiny coral polyps to thrive and build immense coral reefs.

As you drive across the state to various dive sites, take some time to appreciate the stark contrasts in life and topography. Texas' diving is as diverse as its land and, because there's no place like Texas, that's saying a lot.

How To Use This Guide

Even if you own your own compressor and have a lake in your backyard, diving at any level of expertise requires a certain amount of preparation. This guide describes the most popular dive sites in Texas and provides information necessary for planning safe and enjoyable dives.

The dive sites are grouped under three general diving areas: inland, coastal, and offshore. Read the introduction to the area you plan to dive. It describes particular diving requirements, safety tips, and other information that may not be included under your specific destination. At each site, information on location, closest air, and accommodations is given, along with specific diving facts such as water temperature, depth range, hazards, and current conditions.

Before embarking on a long-awaited dive trip, check out your gear and contact a dive shop near the site to get the latest diving and weather conditions (see pages 77–80). There is an equipment checklist on page 81 to make sure you don't forget anything important, and maps on pages 82–89 show parks and campgrounds near the various inland dive sites.

Definition of Ratings

Always rate your diving skills conservatively. Remember the adage that there are old divers and bold divers, but few old, bold divers. We consider a *novice diver* to be someone in decent physical condition who has recently completed a basic diving certification course, or is a certified diver who has not been diving recently, or who has no experience in similar waters. We consider an *intermediate diver* to be a certified diver in excellent physical condition who has been diving actively for at least a year following certification in a basic diving course, and who has been diving recently in similar waters. We consider an *advanced diver* to be someone who has completed an advanced certification diving course, or who has the equivalent experience, has been diving recently in similar waters, has been diving frequently for at least two years, and is in excellent physical condition.

The rating of a site is always based on normal water conditions. When water conditions change, so does your level of expertise. A serene river appropriate for novice divers can suddenly become a raging torrent after heavy rains. A quick call to a dive shop may save you time and money if conditions are hazardous.

2

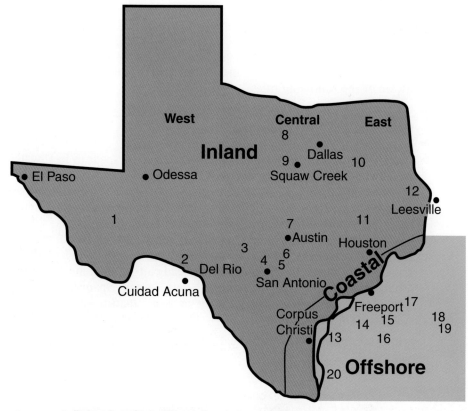

1. Balmorhea State Recreation Area, page 7
2. Lake Amistad, page 12
3. Frio River, page 15
4. Canyon Lake, page 17
5. Comal River, page 19
6. San Marcos River/Aquarena Springs, page 21
7. Lake Travis, page 24
8. Possum Kingdom, page 27
9. Squaw Creek, page 30
10. Athens Scuba Park, page 31
11. Blue Lagoon, page 33
12. Toledo Bend, page 37
13. Jetties, page 40
14. Oil Rigs, page 46
15. *V.A. Fogg*, page 51
16. Liberty Ships, page 54
17. Stetson Bank, page 55
18. Flower Gardens, page 60
19. Mobil H.I. 389, page 67
20. Seven and One-Half Fathom Reef, page 70

*See pages 82–89 for maps of parks/campgrounds near inland dive sites.

Spearfishing Regulations

The Texas Department of Parks and Wildlife strictly regulates freshwater and saltwater fishing. Lakes and marinas are frequently patrolled, so be aware of the following rules:

▶ Spearfishing requires a fishing license. A saltwater stamp is necessary for coastal and offshore fishing.
▶ It is unlawful to leave an edible or bait fish to die.
▶ Only nongame fish may be caught by speargun or spear in freshwater or saltwater. The following may **not** be spearfished:
  Freshwater game fish: blue catfish, brown trout, channel catfish, crappie (black and white), flathead catfish, Guadalupe bass, largemouth bass, red drum, rainbow trout, smallmouth bass, spotted bass, striped bass, walleye, white bass, and hybrids or subspecies of the above.
  Saltwater game fish: blue catfish, blue marlin, broadbill swordfish, brown trout, channel catfish, cobia, flathead catfish, king mackerel, red drum, rainbow trout, sailfish, sauger, shark, snook, Spanish mackerel, spotted seatrout, tarpon, wahoo, walleye, white marlin, and hybrids or subspecies of the above.

For further information, call the Texas Parks and Wildlife Department at 800-792-1112.

Athens Scuba Park (see page 31) is not a Cozumel or Cayman Island, but its $15/day cost and variety of diving activities make it a reasonable and much cheaper alternative. (Photo: Deborah Fugitt)

1

Inland Diving

If you look at a road map of Texas, you'll find a dense web of roadways and towns in east and central Texas. About a thumb's width left of San Antonio, it all evaporates, leaving a few wispy strands to stretch into the empty vastness of West Texas. The picture's basically the same for diving locations. Even though Texas has 5,024 square miles of inland waterways (second only to Alaska), most are in the eastern half of the state. Only three of the twenty sites in this guide lie west of San Antonio, but they are well worth the trip. The cleansing action of water moving through porous, underground rocks and shallow, fast-flowing rivers produces exceptional clarity.

The diversity of inland diving encompasses rivers, lakes, and springs. Without question, spring-fed rivers and lakes offer the finest water conditions. Balmorhea and the Frio, San Marcos, and Comal Rivers are perpetually filled with crystalline water at consistent 70° to 72°F temperatures. The lakes are actually reservoirs, pooling water from the "big" rivers—the Rio Grande, Colorado, Brazos, and Sabine. Although visibility in the lakes varies widely, their depth and their diversity of plants and wildlife are big attractions. Most life can be found in the top 30 feet, although a few have deep sunken forests. Nearly all the lakes have sunken boats, cars, and other objects to explore.

Tips for Inland Diving

Wetsuits. We recommend wearing a full wetsuit or jumpsuit when drift-diving in rivers to avoid injury from rocks and branches. Most divers also wear wetsuits in spring-fed waters, especially when outside temperatures are 60°F or less.

Knives. As a general rule, carry a knife when diving in lakes so you can free yourself from any entanglements with vegetation or monofilament.

Crowds. Dive on a weekday, if at all possible. On weekends and holidays, most of the lakes and rivers attract large numbers of boats, water-skiers, jet skiers, tubers, and fishermen, and this has a marked effect on visibility. Tubers are pretty harmless and can provide some entertaining views from ten feet below. Just remember to look up before you surface.

Although the Blue Lagoon caters primarily to scuba classes, it is also open for recreational diving (see page 33).

Hazards

Dams. Avoid them, especially the turbochannels and spillways.

Caves. There are a variety of caves, grottos, loops, and shoots in the lakes, especially along cliffs. Novices have no business going inside caves. They can be deathtraps for even the most experienced divers. This guide does not list places that don't have enough room for a diver to turn around.

Heavy rains. Rivers can become deep and fast-flowing after heavy rains. Unless you are an exceptionally strong swimmer, wait a few days until the water calms down.

Closest town/air:	Balmorhea/Desert Oasis Dive Shop (next door)
Winter/summer water temperature:	72°F–76°F year-round
Typical depth range:	3–25 feet
Typical water conditions:	Calm
Visibility:	40–80 feet
Expertise required:	Novice
Access:	Concrete walkway (see map on page 82)

Deep in the heart of West Texas, where heat turns highways into molten ribbons and the scrubby creosote bush of the Chihuahuan desert casts a mere few inches of shade, San Solomon Spring bubbles forth an amazing 20 million gallons of pure spring water every day. The spring erupts at Balmorhea State Recreation Area, an oasis set among the foothills of the Davis Mountains four miles west of Balmorhea on Highway 17.

Here you'll find the best freshwater diving in Texas. A 1.75-acre pool, touted as the world's largest spring-fed swimming pool, was constructed around the spring in 1935 by the Civilian Conservation Corps. The pool is designed in a 215-foot diameter circle over the spring. Concrete covers the first 4 to 7 feet around the pool, then moss-covered rocks slope down

Balmorhea is the most misleading diving destination in Texas. Its surface appearance belies a wonderland of bubbling springs, numerous fish, and sparkling waters.

Catfish and Mexican tetras abound in the pool's azure blue waters.

San Solomon Spring bubbles forth at several areas of the pool. The boiling sand attracts many small fish looking for food.

to a bottom depth of 25 feet. The bottom consists of rocks and a bubbling sandy area where the spring emerges.

Balmorhea may look like an ordinary swimming pool, but beneath the surface you'll discover that the extraordinary visibility and diverse wildlife

Mexican tetras go into a feeding frenzy when divers and snorkelers bring down morsels of food.

Balmorhea appears larger than its actual size because of its visibility, which often exceeds 80 feet.

rival Florida's springs. Bring some morsels down and you'll be surrounded by Mexican tetras and catfish. But beware—the tetras nibble on *anything*.

You may see two endangered fish species, the Comanche Springs pupfish and the Pecos mosquitofish, along with minnows, perch, catfish, crayfish, and turtles.

Balmorhea offers a very controlled diving environment, which makes it a popular spot for open-water certification. Park officials regulate activities at the pool to accommodate both swimmers and divers. You may not dive in the nearby canals or in Lake Balmorhea. The pool is open to divers and swimmers year-round from 8:00 a.m. to 10:00 p.m. daily. Every diver must have completed a dive class or review class, logged actual time underwater within the previous 18 months, or be under the supervision of a licensed dive instructor. Current certification cards and up-to-date log books must be presented before signing a liability release. Absolutely no diver may dive alone.

Blue gill perch are the inland counterpart of Texas' offshore and reef fish.

Balmorhea is at least an eight-hour drive from Houston or Dallas, so plan your trip accordingly. Accommodations at the recreation area include campsites, trailer hook-ups, bathing facilities, and an 18-room motel. A concession stand is open during the summer months. We suggest you call well in advance for reservations at the motel, and request current diving regulations before traveling to Balmorhea. Call the Desert Oasis Dive Shop at 915-375-2572 for information about airtank refills, dive equipment sales, and rentals. Call 512-389-8900 or 800-792-1112 (Texas Parks and Wildlife Department) for advance reservations. For inquiries about reservations up to 48 hours in advance, call the Balmorhea Park office at 915-375-2370. For more information, contact the Park Superintendent, Balmorhea State Recreation Area, P.O. Box 15, Toyahvale, Texas 78786.

Closest town/air:	Del Rio/Lake Amistad
Winter/summer water temperature:	62°F/85°F
Typical depth range:	20–80 feet
Typical water conditions:	Slight current at edge of river channels
Visibility:	Averages 12 feet; can reach 35 feet from April to June
Expertise required:	Novice
Access:	Rocky hills, beaches, and boats (see map on page 83)

Covering 64,500 acres, this flood pool at the confluence of the Rio Grande, Pecos, and Devils Rivers is a joint project of the United States and Mexico. Amistad Dam, built in 1968, serves as a port of entry between the two countries. A line of buoys down the middle of the lake marks the international boundary line and an opportunity for you honest folks out there who are a little short of funds. Drive a boat past the buoys, jump in the water, take a deep breath, and . . . voila! You can now boast with the best about having been on an international dive trip.

Although there are several access points at Lake Amistad, the limestone shore at Diablo East is the easiest and most popular.

Divers at Lake Amistad can explore rocky pinnacles, cliffs, and sunken objects, including two submerged ranch houses.

No dive shop currently serves the lake. Air is available at American Campgrounds, located less than a mile south of the lake on Highway 90 West. Call 210-775-7491 for more information. Headed out of Del Rio, on the right about one mile before the bridge crossing over the lake, is Diablo East, a large, buoyed-off area with sunken boats, plenty of fish, and grass at 12 feet. In spring, little freshwater jellyfish appear for a couple of weeks. Adjacent to the area are pinnacles with sharp drop-offs. Like wall dives, the pinnacles drop 150 feet into the old river channel. Also at Diablo East are the San Pedro Cliffs, a cove protected from boat traffic and exclusively for divers. Accessible by boat, it consists of cliffs, sheer walls, and small fruit trees at 45 feet.

There are three good beach sites along the shore, as well as sunken cemeteries, railroad tracks, wrecks, and buildings to be explored. Other sites include an old sunken ranch house at Castle Canyon, Indian Springs in the Devils River arm, and the old sunken Highway 277 bridge running

Lake Amistad's small fish seek protection among the lake grasses near the shore.

across San Pedro Canyon. On the Mexican side, there are fewer facilities, but diving is just as good and includes another sunken ranch up the Rio Grande arm.

Amistad offers some of the clearest lake diving in the state, partly because the reservoir is relatively new. Grass and tree decomposition have not yet affected water clarity, although visibility can decrease during hot, dry weather because of algae blooms.

Numerous camping and boat rental facilities surround the lake. Del Rio is 12 miles downstream of the dam on U.S. 90, and the small, colorful town of Cuidad Acuna, Mexico is less than 10 miles west of Del Rio. Passports or automobile permits are not required to go into Cuidad Acuna. For further information, contact the National Park Service, Amistad Recreation Area at 210-775-7491.

Closest town/air:	Uvalde/San Antonio
Winter/summer water temperature:	62°F/72°F
Typical depth range:	Shallow bed to 18 feet
Typical water conditions:	Generally mild, possible surge currents after heavy rains
Visibility:	10–20 feet
Expertise required:	Novice
Access:	Rocky, dirt banks (see map on page 84)

Frio means "cold" in Spanish, and you'll probably need a full wetsuit to dive here. Clear spring water feeds the Frio River from the Edwards Aquifer recharge zone. Most of the river is only three to four feet deep and lined with large, moss-covered rocks and boulders. The deeper, diveable portions of the river extend 20 miles along predominantly private property, so access is very limited.

Garner State Park, 31 miles north of Uvalde on U.S. 83, lies along a 1½ mile stretch of the river that has several pools ranging from 15 to 20 feet deep. Catfish, perch, bass, and carp are common here.

One of the few public access points for diving the Frio River is at Garner State Park. Below the spillway, several 15-foot depressions house schools of catfish, largemouth bass, and perch.

Numerous large boulders and a variety of aquatic plants decorate the cool, clear waters of the Frio.

The crowds pack into Garner on holidays and daily during June, July, and August. Tubers often float down from the spillway at the north end of the park. Plan to spend a few days enjoying the scenery. The park is nestled in a scenic valley surrounded by high hills and cliffs that offer some spectacular panoramic views. Camping, showers, and cabin rentals are available. Reservations for campsites are needed up to 11 months in advance. For more information, contact the Park Superintendent, Garner State Park, Concan, Texas 78838, or call 210-232-6132.

Closest city/air:	New Braunfels/The Sundowner Dive Shop (just past Jacobs Creek)
Winter/summer water temperature:	48°F/80°F
Typical depth range:	20–80 feet
Typical water conditions:	Calm
Visibility:	8–25 feet
Expertise required:	Novice
Access:	Rocky limestone shore (see map on page 85)

Canyon Lake lies 20 miles northeast of New Braunfels on FM 306. Steep-shouldered, evergreen hills surround this scenic 8,250-acre lake that abounds with largemouth bass, catfish, and blue gill perch. You'll probably need a wetsuit below the thermoclines, which sit at about 20 and 40 feet in the summer.

The most accessible dive spots are North Park, Comal Park, and Overlook Park. To reach North Park, turn left at the Sundowner Lounge from FM

The clearest near-shore water at Canyon Lake is at Overlook Park. The bottom plummets 100 feet from a short ledge into the old Guadalupe River channel.

A diver pauses at the end of a ledge at Overlook Park prior to descending a 100-foot limestone wall.

306. The road leads to the edge of the lake, but you'll need to carry your gear about 50 yards. The silt and gravel bottom gradually slopes to three wrecked cars and a boat between 20 and 40 feet, and a forest at 60 to 80 feet.

Comal Park is on the opposite side of the lake from North Park. Turn left on 2673 from FM 306 and go about nine miles to Canyon Park Drive, turning right at the Circle-K gas station. Turn right again on Grandview, then left on Canyon Lake Forest. The entrance to Comal Park is the first right off Canyon Lake Forest. Here you can explore the ledges of the wall that drops to 90 feet about 20 feet from shore.

The best diving is at Overlook Park, across the dam from North Park. A steep hill leads to the shore. The bottom drops from 3 feet to 100 feet into the old Guadalupe River bottom, with treetops at 70 to 80 feet.

North Park has minimal camping facilities. Other lakeside accommodations can be found at Jacobs Creek, Canyon Lake, and Potters Creek Parks, or you may want to contact The Bunkhaus at 210-935-2735 or Canyon Lake Cottages at 210-964-3621. The Sundowner Dive Shop can be reached at 210-964-2112.

Comal River 5

Closest town/air:	New Braunfels/Canyon Lake
Winter/summer water temperature:	72°F year-round
Typical depth range:	15 feet maximum
Typical water conditions:	Minimal current, possible surge after heavy rains
Visibility:	5–35 feet
Expertise required:	Novice
Access:	Grassy and concrete embankments

Comal Springs feed the four-mile long Comal River, which flows through the heart of New Braunfels. Like the San Marcos, the river contains shallow depths which make it a good snorkeling spot. The bottom consists of flat, white limestone slabs and silt with sparse vegetation. You'll see catfish, bass, perch, carp and freshwater prawn. Diving is divided into three areas—upper Comal, middle Comal, and lower Comal.

The Comal River winds through the heart of New Braunfels and provides a variety of recreational activities.

The most commonly seen fish in the Comal is the blue gill perch.

The upper Comal lies along Hinman Island at Landa Park. Landa Street will take you to the main entrance of the park. Turn right on Hinman Island Drive, which runs parallel to the river. Don't plan to dive the upper Comal on weekends. The gates to Hinman Island Drive are locked then, and you'll have to carry your gear about ¼ mile from the nearest parking area. Chances are you'll encounter more tubers than wildlife here.

Walk around the Tube Shoot and enter the water at the North Seguin Bridge to dive the middle Comal. It takes about an hour to dive this section. You can exit at the Coll Street Bridge or continue on into the lower Comal.

The lower Comal provides the best diving. It is the longest and deepest part of the river and may take more than an hour to complete, even though on land it only extends the length of Coll Street. Stairs are available at the Coll Street Bridge, and public parking is less than a block away. Make plans to have someone drive your car to the exit at the end of Coll Street. The end of this street is the *last* public exit ("Last Tube Shoot"). Get out here, or you'll take a freefall over a small dam a little further downstream.

Tubers represent the worst and best aspects of diving the Comal. When they're out in large numbers, visibility can decrease to as little as five feet. They also tend to lose things in the water (like jewelry and money), and this makes the river a great place to treasure hunt. The Gulf Coast Council of Diving Clubs hosts an annual "Trash Fest" at Hinman Island each October. Prizes are awarded to divers collecting the most trash from the river.

Accommodations are available in New Braunfels. Landa Park does not provide overnight camping. The closest air is available at Goofy's Store on Canyon Lake, located about ten miles from the Comal River on FM 306.

Closest town/air:	San Marcos/on site
Winter/summer water temperature:	72°F year-round
Typical depth range:	3–25 feet
Typical water conditions:	Calm, possible surge currents after heavy rains
Visibility:	25–80 feet
Expertise required:	Novice/Intermediate (35 hours minimum required for Aquarena Springs)
Access:	Concrete bank and sandy grass

Exceptional clarity and diverse wildlife make the San Marcos the best river dive in the state. More endangered species may live in the San Marcos River than in any other freshwater body in Texas. The river begins at Spring Lake in Aquarena Springs, which is itself in the throes of a battle for survival. Continued drought in the Edwards Aquifer recharge zone and pumping of water by San Antonio for municipal uses is affecting water pressure at the springs. The clear, cool water we see here today may soon be altered, diminishing the springs' beauty and abundance of wildlife.

The cool, clear water and abundant aquatic life of the San Marcos River attract divers, snorkelers, and underwater photographers.

The best diving is accessed just beyond the spillway from Spring Lake in front of Pepper's Restaurant, and proceeds for ¾ mile to Rio Vista Park at I.H. 35. Some people prefer to enter the water from the concrete banks at Sewall Park, a short distance downstream from Pepper's. Water depth ranges from only three to eight feet up to Rio Vista Park, so you can enjoy the scenery equally well by just snorkeling. The water deepens to 15 feet at Rio Vista Park.

The San Marcos River teems with life. Forty different varieties of fresh-water plants cover the bottom, including the rare and endangered Texas

Rare and endangered species find refuge in the beautiful San Marcos. The giant freshwater prawn, which can measure 20 inches long, usually hides during the day but can easily be seen at night.

wild rice, found only in the San Marcos. You'll also see bass, giant mollies, Rio Grande and blue gill perch, catfish, turtles, Mexican tetras, and possibly even the endangered fountain darter, blind salamander, gambusia, and San Marcos salamander. Renegade goldfish appear once or twice a year, when semesters end at Southwest Texas State University. Night dives may bring out freshwater eels, red crawfish, and the giant freshwater prawn, which measures up to 20 inches in length.

Aquarena Springs, located above the dam, offers the best freshwater diving in the state. Fed by several springs that bubble up from a sandy bottom, the basin provides exceptional visibility. Towering stands of aquatic plants create a luxuriant "kelp-forest" type backdrop for albino catfish, huge spotted gar, Rio Grande perch, and swarms of Mexican tetras. To protect this pristine and rare habitat, diving is allowed only on a *highly* restricted basis. Only experienced divers booked through an approved dive shop are permitted access. All divers receive an environmental impact briefing and are accompanied by both a dive master and a tour guide. Prices for dive packages range from $35 to $220, with one day and overnight dives available. Call Aquarena Springs Resort (512-245-7595) for a list of approved dive shops and other information.

Texas wild rice can be viewed in several shallow areas of the river. This plant, found nowhere else in the world, is on the verge of extinction, and its existence is directly tied to the well-being of the river.

Closest town/air:	Austin/Lake Travis
Winter/summer water	
temperature:	60°F/85°F
Typical depth range:	20–70 feet
Typical water conditions:	Calm to slightly choppy
Visibility:	10–25 feet
Expertise required:	Novice to Intermediate
Access:	Rocky shore or boat (see map on page 86)

Lake Travis is one of the Highland lakes that stair-step up the Colorado River just outside of Austin. Someone caught a 200-pound catfish here several years ago, or so the story goes. Believe it or not, catfish "the size of a man or even a small car" *do* live in the 150-foot plus depths of the old river channel. Whiskered friends aside, Lake Travis is tremendously popular for a few other reasons, like its beautiful setting among rolling hills, bikini-clad coeds from the University of Texas, romantic midnight sails, and impressive lakefront properties. On top of all this are its numerous and varied dive sites.

Hill country scenery and diversity of dive sites make Lake Travis the most frequently dived lake in the state.

Some access points consist of steep rock ledges, so many divers prefer to gear up in the water.

Windy Point Park, open year-round (except Thanksgiving and Christmas Day), offers easy access to the lake for both sport diving and dive training. The park provides carts to roll dive gear up to the lake's edge, an underwater contour map of Windy Point, and concrete steps down to the water. The dive area is buoyed off 200 feet out into the water. From 30 feet down, you'll see a number of wrecked boats and cars, as well as a gallery of whimsical metal sculptures. A series of drop-offs extends down to a sunken forest of pecan trees from 90 to 110 feet.

Other sites are best accessed by boat. The northwest side of Starnes Island gradually slopes to 100 feet, with sunken boats at 25 and 60 feet. The area is buoyed off and offers several underwater platforms for dive classes. For more experienced divers, the other side of the island has good wall diving over the old Colorado River bed. The Walls at Marshall Ford Park drop in 50-foot increments into some of the deepest and clearest water in the lake. An interesting dive between Hippy Hollow and Marshall Ford Park is the old shaker plant from the construction of the dam. Diving here extends to 110 feet, and you'll see concrete pillars and pads and truck remnants. Night dives at Hippy Hollow include feeding white and black bass. Overnight camping, showers, and cooking grills are available.

To reach the park from the intersection of 620 at 2222, go northwest one mile on Bullick Hollow. Proceed to the next intersection and turn left at Oasis Bluff. Go .6 miles to Comanche Trail and turn right. Drive 1.9 miles past Travis County's Hippy Hollow and Bob Wentz parks to the intersection of Comanche Trail and Ridgetop Terrace. Turn left. The park

Silt-covered boulders line the sides and bottom of Lake Travis, along with occasional submerged forests. Commonly seen fish are blue gill perch, Rio Grande perch, catfish, and buffalo carp.

entrance is on the immediate right. For more information, contact Windy Point Park at 512-266-DEEP.

Also located on the east shore (on Comanche Trail) is Lake Travis Scuba Park, a site designed primarily for dive students. This protected dive training area and underwater playground extends 100 yards from shore to a depth of 60 feet, accessed by a 15,000-square-foot floating dock. Underwater, dive instructors, students, and recreational divers can explore several boat wrecks or hand feed blue gill perch and arm-length catfish. All divers must be under the direct supervision of a licensed, insured instructor or dive master. A floating museum, underwater observation room, gift shop, heated shelter for winter diving, scuba rental, gear transport, equipment storage, and overnight camping facilities add to the park's creature comforts. For more information, contact Lake Travis Scuba Park at 512-266-2933.

We recommend wearing a wetsuit below 60 feet during the summer. Beware of boaters and jet skiers on weekends and holidays, especially outside the buoys of Windy Point Park. Minimal camping is also available at the Lower Colorado River Authority (LCRA) park near Mansfield Dam, with additional accommodations in Austin.

Closest town/air:	Graford/Lake Possum Kingdom
Winter/summer water	
temperature:	55°F/82°F
Typical depth range:	10–100 feet
Typical water conditions:	Calm
Visibility:	5–20 feet
Expertise required:	Novice
Access:	Concrete, sandy beach, and boat (see map on page 87)

Lake Possum Kingdom covers 20,000 acres amid mesquite and junipers in the rocky canyons of the Palo Pinto Mountains. It was created with the construction of the Morris Sheppard Dam on the Brazos River in the late 1940's, and numerous quiet coves dot its 310-mile shoreline. Even before you see a road sign, you'll know this has got to be a "possum somewhere" because of the unbelievable number of possums.

Only one full-service dive shop, Scuba Point, sits on the lake. It has a ramp, three pier docks, and a large area (250 × 300 feet) buoyed off in front of the shop. It boasts the world's largest dive-shop compressor, nick-named "goldfinger," which was previously used in a commercial oxygen

Lake Possum Kingdom was created in the late 1940's with the construction of the Morris Sheppard Dam. The main shore diving area is near Scuba Point, the only dive shop on the lake.

Divers can explore numerous sunken objects near shore, as well as a variety of natural formations in deeper water.

At Scuba Point divers may enter the water directly from one of the three pier docks or arrange to be picked up for a boat dive.

plant. The buoyed area in front has a gently sloping bottom with a variety of sunken objects for spatial reference. Be very careful of boat traffic when surfacing near the pier docks.

Boat access to other dive sites can be arranged through the dive shop. The Walls are cliffs that extend 80 to 100 feet into the water. Here you can explore along two rock ledges and watch catfish and striped bass. The Cove is full of trees and grass, with a flat bottom to about 50 feet, then a drop-off to 85 feet.

Though diving is available year-round, May through Labor Day comprises the busiest season. Scuba Point is closed from the end of November through mid-March. Weekend hours are 9:00 a.m. until 7:00 p.m. Weekday hours are 10:00 a.m. until 8:00 p.m., but closing time often extends "until the customers are too tired or their money runs out."

Scuba Point provides free camping facilities. Restaurants, motels, grocery stores, and other amenities are available in the community of Possum Kingdom. Cabins and a grocery store are also available at Possum Kingdom Recreation Area, located 45 miles away on the other side of the lake. For more information, call the dive shop at 817-779-2482 or the recreation area at 817-549-1803.

Closest town/air:	Granbury
Winter/summer water temperature:	60°F/95°F
Typical depth range:	To 125 feet (by the dam)
Typical water conditions:	Calm
Visibility:	5–15 feet
Expertise required:	Novice
Access:	Restricted to designated areas or boat

Squaw Creek lies halfway between Granbury and Glen Rose off Highway 144, 45 miles southwest of Ft. Worth. It was constructed in 1977 by Texas Utilities as a cooling pond for a nuclear power plant being built at the site. The plant became operational in 1991. Though short on underwater structure, the lake offers haven for hybrid bass. Squaw Creek Park is the only public access to the lake and has facilities for fishing, swimming, and camping. Closest air is seven miles away at Outdoor Adventurers (817-573-3426). The park strictly regulates activities, with diving permitted from 6:00 a.m. until sundown. No night diving is allowed. The park is closed every Tuesday and Wednesday. Before diving here, call Texas Utilities at 817-573-7053 for updates on diving conditions and regulations.

Divers take a surface interval at Squaw Creek.

Closest town/air:	Athens/on site
Winter/summer water temperature:	47°F/90°F
Typical depth range:	26–35 feet
Typical water conditions:	Calm
Visibility:	2–50 feet
Expertise required:	Novice
Access:	Bank or platform

Located in downtown Athens, the park is built on the site of an old quarry. This spring-fed lake is accessed by a selection of wooden platforms situated within easy walking distance of the parking area and features a cornucopia of underwater objects: boats, tour buses, a piano, an airplane, a motorcycle, and simulated caves. Lots of fish, including largemouth bass exceeding two feet, enliven the scenery. Regularly scheduled treasure hunts, poker games, and navigation races add to the fun. Facilities include a dive shop, tent campsites, showers, picnic areas, a new restaurant, and a stage for live bands. Cost for diving (including a night dive) is $15 per person, with lower rates for nondivers. The lake is closed from December through February, but the park is open to visitors year-round. For more information call 903-675-5762.

Largemouth bass are commonly seen in the old quarry; some are over two feet long. (Photo: Deborah Fugitt)

Closest town/air:	Huntsville/Blue Lagoon
Winter/summer water temperature:	60°F/90°F
Typical depth range:	15–35 feet
Typical water conditions:	Calm
Visibility:	5–60 feet
Expertise required:	Novice
Access:	Sandy beach and rocks (see map on page 88)

You may have heard of Texas' own "Cozumel in the Pines." This privately owned, 100-acre site lies 6 miles northeast of Huntsville (70 miles north of Houston) among the towering pines of the Sam Houston National Forest. It was opened in 1986 as an open water training facility for scuba divers. The Blue Lagoon consists of two quartzite quarries, each about six acres, fed by artesian springs. The clear, Caribbean-like blue water provides visibility second only to Balmorhea in West Texas. Its low pH discourages growth of bacteria and vegetation. The only species to

Both lagoons contain sunken boats. One of the highlights of Lagoon I is exploring the 40-foot Chris Craft.

◄ *The spring-fed lake at Athens Scuba Park contains schools of blue gill perch, as well as numerous submerged objects. (Photo: Deborah Fugitt)*

Located near Huntsville, the Blue Lagoon consists of two flooded quartzite quarries. The water's low pH discourages algal growth, contributing to visibility exceeding 50 feet.

Alternating silty areas and rocky outcroppings form the bottom terrain of both lagoons.

observe are the dragonfly nymph, which looks and acts like a shrimp, and an "as yet to be identified" type of fish, recently introduced to the lagoon.

The Blue Lagoon offers the best easy dive in Texas and attracts more than 15,000 visitors annually. It's the perfect spot to fine-tune diving skills, practice underwater photography, and check out equipment. Maximum depth is 35 feet. To preserve visibility, ten underwater platforms were constructed at 25–30 feet to reduce disturbance of the silty bottom during dive classes. The platforms also enable dive instructors to congregate with students and see the whole group at one time.

Both Lagoons I and II have beautiful, jagged cliffs that extend 20 feet below the water surface. Divers can see both boulders the size of cars and large boats at each site. Lagoon I also boasts a sunken airplane. Every

Weekend visitors find the Blue Lagoon an excellent place to enjoy night diving.

Halloween, the boats are converted into "haunted boats" with hidden skeletons, pumpkins, and sharks.

The Blue Lagoon caters only to divers. Swimming is allowed only for guests of divers, and boating is prohibited. Amenities include on-site camping, picnic tables with barbeque pits, and bagged ice. Meals and additional accommodations are just 15 minutes away in Huntsville. The Blue Lagoon is open seven days a week from mid-May through September (this can vary) and on weekends during other months. Daily admission charges are $10.00 for divers and $5.00 for nondivers. For directions and additional information, call the Blue Lagoon at 409-291–6111.

Closest town/air:	Leesville, Louisiana (20 miles)
Winter/summer water temperature:	53°F/82°F
Typical depth range:	20–60 feet
Typical water conditions:	Variable
Visibility:	10 feet
Expertise required:	Novice
Access:	Sandy beach (see map on page 89)

Ask someone on the east side of Toledo Bend where the Cajun gators are and he'll say, "De otre side." Ask someone on the west side of Toledo Bend where the Texas-size gators are and he'll say "T'othur side." No one claims them, and few have actually seen them, but they're here.

Toledo Bend Reservoir is on the Sabine River on the Texas-Louisiana border. The water is clear, but tea-colored from leaf decomposition, and packed with fish and vegetation. A 15-to-20-foot-wide strip of grass grows 20 feet from the shore. The bottom is sandy silt covered with logs and limbs. You'll find red crawfish, freshwater clams, catfish, bass, and

On-site parking and terraces make the north side of the dam the best access point at Toledo Bend.

Tannic acid from plant decomposition gives the water at Toledo Bend its unique coloration. A variety of grasses, some 15 feet tall, can be explored adjacent to the dam.

perch. Because of the vegetation and number of fishermen here, it is essential that you dive with a knife.

The best access and facilities are on the Louisiana side. From Burkville, Texas, take 692 north for 14 miles to Coffer Dam. The water is buoyed off about 20 feet away from the parking area at the end of the dam. A check-out platform, sunken cars, and other objects are within the buoys. Divers should avoid the floodgates that are a short distance north of the dive area.

Numerous islands are accessible by boat and generally have clearer water than exists along the shore. Most of the property on the Texas side is privately owned, but can be dived by boat. This water is deeper and has underwater cliffs about 100 yards from shore.

Camping is available at numerous lakeside locations in Louisiana. Toledo Bend lies on the outskirts of the Big Thicket, and the heat and humidity can be uncomfortable in the summer. You may want to look into other accommodations in Leesville. For further information, contact the Sabine River Authority in Many, Louisiana at 318-256-4112 or the Sabine Parish Tourist and Recreation Commission at 800-358-7802.

2

Coastal Diving

The coastline of Texas extends 624 miles from Louisiana to Mexico. Practically all of it is sandy beach, which is great for beachcombers but unfortunately leaves few decent diving areas. The nearshore waters of the Gulf of Mexico carry a large amount of sediment in suspension, making visibility a couple of feet at most. If you swim out from shore to avoid breaking waves, you run into an area of unpredictable rip tides and undertows. Because of the phenomenally persistent brown tide invasion, the once pristine Laguna Madre, which still offers winsurfers plenty of fun, no longer provides sufficient visibility to attract divers. Only one site remains that is comparatively safe, offers acceptable visibility, and harbors interesting marine life.

Although "brown tides" have severely reduced underwater visibility in Laguna Madre, windsurfers love its brisk winds and snorkelers its shallow water.

Closest town/air:	Port Aransas
Winter/summer water temperature:	55°F/86°F
Typical depth range:	10–30 feet
Typical water conditions:	Variable; currents can be very strong
Visibility:	3–20 feet
Expertise required:	Intermediate
Access:	Rocks

The jetties extend Gulfward from Port Aransas at the northern tip of Mustang Island. Take the ferry from S.H. 136 across Aransas Pass to Port Aransas, or take Park Road 53 from Padre Island. Parking is available on the beach at the south jetty, and a jetty ferry leaves every ½ hour to the north jetty.

The jetties are rocky mounds ½ mile apart and one mile long, with the last ¼ mile under water. The rocky rubble extends down about 20 feet to a sandy bottom. Visibility peaks from late summer to early fall and is best on a daily basis between 10:00 a.m. and 2:00 p.m., when the sun is at its highest angle.

Rocks located beneath the low tide line are thickly covered with marine algaes. It is advisable for buddies to help each other gear up while on these slippery rocks.

The marine algaes attached to the rocks are plants and grow in myriad forms and colors.

Most diving and snorkeling at the Aransas Pass jetties occur close to the island. The waters are more protected here, and there are usually fewer fishermen.

Algae, barnacles, sea urchins, and encrusting sponges cover the rocks, and the water is full of marine tropicals. Seeing octopus, barracuda, and sharks is not unusual, and spearfishing is popular. If you're interested in diving away from the jetties, you can follow one of the three lateral spurs that extend under water about 100 yards into the channel.

There are numerous hazards that divers should be aware of when diving the jetties: (1) Fishermen line the south jetty at 2-foot intervals on weekends. Use a dive flag and a knife, or go over to the north jetty where there are fewer crowds; (2) The currents here are unpredictable and can be very strong during tide changes; (3) Wear gloves and wetsuit (or some other cover) to protect against the barnacle-encrusted rocks. Passing water traffic creates waves that can throw you around; (4) Be careful of boat traffic when diving near the channel on days of low visibility; (5) Lastly, this is the site of the annual Texas Shark Fishing Contest. These aren't shark-infested waters, but if you're planning a night dive, remember their presence.

There is a wide selection of accommodations and dive shops in Port Aransas and Corpus Christi.

3

Offshore Diving

The Gulf of Mexico presents a unique diving environment. In other areas of the world, most open ocean diving consists of atolls and barrier reefs situated within reasonable proximity to land. Until recent years, all Gulf dive sites lay in deep water up to 120 miles from shore, where divers were subjected to the full force of currents and unpredictable weather. Truly "open" ocean diving, the Gulf was once solely a destination for divers with intermediate-level expertise or more.

However, thanks to the development of the Artificial Reef Program, a cooperative effort between the Texas Parks and Wildlife Department, the Texas Department of Transportation, and private industries, the Gulf now boasts 26 total dive sites that consist of either one or more sunken vessels, gigantic blocks formed from coal ash, discarded oil rig jackets, or a combination of these features. One of these—the Port Isabel/South Padre Island Artificial Reef Site—is an easy one-day dive. Located less than ten miles offshore, this already popular marine playground offers a sunken tugboat and two rig jackets at depths less than 80 feet.

If you've never dived offshore, the sheer number and diversity of wildlife will astound you. The flat and featureless floor of the Gulf makes any type of underwater structure a mecca for marine life seeking hard substrate, shelter, and food. Whether natural or artificial, the Gulf dive sites display beautiful and fascinating communities of interdependent life.

On a conservation note, corals should be treated with care and respect. Despite a dense, brittle exoskeleton, coral polyps are soft and delicate, with little or no defense against poking and finning. Damaged polyps release symbiotic zooxanthellae (algae) out of their bodies and eventually die. One diver hurting one little polyp is not a tragedy, but hundreds of divers destroying hundreds of polyps is. A good adage to follow: "Take only memories (or pictures) and leave behind only bubbles."

Warm water and calmer weather make summer and fall the best seasons to dive offshore. Visibility is generally good close to shore, but can vary with the movement of plankton and sediment by nearshore currents. It can reach 125 feet at the Flower Gardens near the edge of the outer continental shelf. We strongly recommend that you make reservations a few months in advance of your planned trip. Some dive boats have all their weekends booked by the beginning of the dive season. Because of the distances

Many offshore destinations are more than forty miles from shore. Larger vessels, specifically rigged for diving, are usually required to make these trips safe and enjoyable.

involved, you may get the chance to dive a variety of sites in the Gulf (an oil rig, the Flower Gardens, Stetson Bank) on the same excursion. Many dive operations are available for booking; Flinn Charters of Lake Jackson is the most experienced. However, all reservations are arranged through dive shops, with those located near the coast having the best access to dive boats and offshore diving information.

Tips for Offshore Diving

Preparation: Make sure all your gear checks out before getting on the boat. Pack some medication if you're prone to seasickness. There's nothing like rolling on the seas for a few hours between dives.

Entry/Exit: As a general rule, you should descend against the current and ascend with the current. You have more air and more energy at the beginning of a dive. Some sites are 50 feet or more below the surface, so follow the anchor line descending and ascending. A safety decompression stop should be made at ten feet before exiting the water.

Wetsuits: These should be worn on all offshore dives, especially at oil rigs.

Spearfishing: Carefully monitor your air supply, depth, and nitrogen status, and don't shoot a fish with less than 1,500 psi in your tank. Because of the size of some of the fish offshore, we recommend adding a shock line to the cable. Dive shops usually sell and install a variety of spearfishing equipment.

Hazards

Orientation: *Never* go under water without a spatial reference point. Descend along rig legs or follow an anchor line all the way down to the site. Maintain a reference point throughout your dive. It doesn't take long at 70 feet to drift a few hundred yards from the dive boat.

Currents: There are some real "rip snorters" in the Gulf. They're not seasonal or predictable and can run to 4 knots.

Attractive and unusual sponge development on offshore structures can be quite distracting, so watch your depth closely.

Nearest point of departure:	Galveston, Freeport, Corpus Christi
Winter/summer water temperature:	65°F/84°F
Typical depth range:	Varies with distance from shore; can exceed 80 feet
Typical water conditions:	Highly variable
Visibility:	Varies with distance from shore; to 100 feet
Expertise required:	Intermediate

Offshore oil platforms are the most abundant form of reef community in the Gulf of Mexico. Hundreds of rigs dot the continental shelf off Texas and Louisiana. The underwater structures of a rig in 100 feet of water typically add 2 acres of hard surface to the water column.

If you're into marine biology, a rig is a fascinating place to explore a vertical marine community. Every square inch is covered by barnacles, encrusting sponges, bryzoans, and the occasional white hydroid or ivory

Large schools of Atlantic spadefish frequently investigate divers exploring the rig structures.

Hundreds of oil rigs dot the Texas coast, extending to the outer continental shelf. Each of these artificial reefs is like an underwater skyscraper or vertical zoo of marine life.

Divers can hand feed many reef denizens. Soapfish and damselfish are easily lured by any type of table scrap.

Numerous small blennies make their homes inside vacant barnacles. They are curious and, if approached slowly, can be viewed at close range.

bush coral. You can observe thousands of plate-sized spadefish schooling near the surface or flounder sifting through the muddy bottom. Soapfish, damselfish, blennies, butterflyfish, and angelfish dart through the maze of pipes and valves, avoiding the predatory jaws of barracuda, large amber-jacks, and groupers.

Rig diving is considered to be the safest type of diving in the Gulf because depth can be controlled. You can dive at 5 feet or 150 feet, depending on how long you want your dive to last. However, you can expect to share a rig with some fishermen. Dive boat captains put up dive flags, and if you stay within the rig structure you're pretty well protected. Exercise some caution when surfacing inside the rig because wave action can throw you against the large, sharp barnacles that cover the rig legs.

The size of a rig can only be appreciated from under water. The legs of these artificial reefs can extend beyond the 200-foot range, and provide the option of multi-level diving.

These are excellent spearfishing sites. Before leaving shore, consult a dive shop for rigging your gun with stainless steel cable (barnacles can sever nylon) and a shock line. Also, don't shoot toward rig structures because they can deflect the spear toward other divers. For more information, contact a coastal dive shop (see page 77).

Nearest point of departure:	Freeport
Winter/summer water temperature:	65°F/84°F
Typical depth range:	65–100 feet
Typical water conditions:	Highly variable
Visibility:	20–100 feet
Expertise required:	Intermediate

Even for divers who frequently visit the *V.A. Fogg,* this wreck evokes a sense of awe and curiosity because of its size and the tragedy that caused such staggering damage and loss of life. The *SS V.A. Fogg* disappeared 33 miles southeast of Freeport on February 1, 1972. The tanker was on its way to Galveston after unloading highly flammable benzene at Freeport. Three hours after its departure from Freeport, an explosion ripped through the hull, killing all 39 crewmen and sinking the 572-foot, 12,500-gross ton

The wreck of the V.A. Fogg *exudes an eerie and mysterious aura that intrigues divers.*

The V.A. Fogg *is a popular fishing spot. A diver examines tangled monofilament around a valve system encrusted with sponges.*

Algae covers a massive anchor chain lying on the bow. ▼

tanker in less than two minutes. When the wreckage was located 12 days later, divers found pieces of steel plating 300 feet from the ship, massive internal damage, and blast marks from mid-ship forward. The condition of the tanker precluded any salvage operations, so the Coast Guard blasted the superstructure to 65 feet to prevent navigation hazards.

Undulating clouds of baitfish scurry in a single flash of silver at the slightest threat.

Today, the *V.A. Fogg* is a highly successful, unplanned artificial reef. She sits in 100 feet of water and is so large that at 80 feet, a diver will see only about one-tenth of the wreck. A carpet of green, brown, and red encrusting algae covers her hull, and clusters of hydroids, soft corals, and ivory bush coral dot the surface. Horned triggerfish, Atlantic spadefish, sergeant-majors, and angelfish roam around, and thousands of baitfish travel in undulating clouds. Commercial fishermen frequent the site for red snapper and bonita, but have to move when dive flags are up.

The ship's interior is dominated by encrusting sponges. We recommend advanced diving skills for interior diving because of the depth and the lack of light. Although most divers don't spend much time inside the hull, you should be reasonably safe using a dive light and a safety line.

Located at the Texas Parks and Wildlife Artificial Reef Program's reef site number 9, the *V.A. Fogg* has been joined in recent years by two Liberty Ships, one welded pipe reef, and a pyramid constructed of 300 giant sized, fly-ash blocks (coal by-product). A prototype for underwater parks of the future, this complex of structures offers a variety of habitats for large numbers of grouper, red snapper, amberjack, shark, and other fascinating marine species.

Nearest point of departure:	Check with your local dive shop
Winter/summer water	
temperature:	65°F/84°F
Typical depth range:	70–100 feet
Typical water conditions:	Variable; currents can be very strong
Visibility:	To 100 feet
Expertise required:	Advanced

Sometimes called "liberty reefs," these 12 surplus WWII Liberty Ships were sunk along the Gulf Coast in 1975 and 1976 to create artificial reefs at six different sites. They feature marine life similar to that found at the *V.A. Fogg,* and the bow of one ship actually sits 20 feet from the bow of this huge, haunting vessel. The ships were sunk in at least 100 feet of water to avoid the soft, muddy bottom near shore. Because of this depth, only more experienced divers should visit the ships. Some ships are accompanied by scrap oil rig jackets, which provide additional structure and underwater habitat for a wide variety of colorful and captivating marine life.

A safety stop at ten feet is recommended whenever diving deep wreck dive locations.

Nearest point of departure:	Freeport
Winter/summer water	
temperature:	65°F/84°F
Typical depth range:	60–90 feet
Typical water conditions:	Highly variable
Visibility:	30–110 feet
Expertise required:	Intermediate

Stetson Bank offers the most exhilarating dive on the Gulf Coast. Lying atop a salt dome in 180 feet of water 70.5 nautical miles southeast of Freeport, the vertically dipping claystones and siltstones form an outline resembling a Stetson hat, hence its name.

(text continued on page 58)

Stetson Bank is frequently described as looking like the surface of the moon. The upper reef area consists of large siltstones and claystones overlain by fire coral and encrusting sponges.

Abundant and diverse fish life attracts divers to this marginal reef.

An underwater photographer pauses to shoot a 9-inch jackknife fish.

The well camouflaged scorpionfish is one of the few real hazards in the sea. Its dorsal spines are poisonous and can cause infection and great pain.

The white-spotted filefish roams the reef, feeding on sponges and fire coral.

A shy, golden-tailed moray peers out from among fire coral and encrusting sponges.

(text continued from page 55)

A standard remark by first-time divers is, "Wow! I can't believe the number of fish down there!" For a marginal reef, Stetson has an amazingly diverse population of marine life. Covered in encrusting sponges and fire coral, the pinnacled surface at 60 to 90 feet swarms with schools of tropical fish and big game fish such as barracuda, amberjack, and grouper. You'll stand a good chance of seeing sharks and giant stingrays. Even whale sharks occasionally visit.

If your dive boat anchors near the edge of the bank, you can set yourself up for a fascinating experience. Take some time to explore the crest,

In a world of blue, the black dots and blue lines on the scrawled filefish help it blend into its environment.

then drift out past the lip and over the edge. The inky black abyss that surrounds the bank seems to pull you down and conjures up some hair-raising and imaginative thoughts. Most divers explore along the walls over the edge, but some like to go out a few feet for a wider view. Keep your distance to a minimum and always maintain eye contact with the bank.

For you hardy souls who want to try a night dive, *spooky* is the word. Remember, whatever hides down in the abyss during the day comes up at night to feed, so keep your dive light and/or camera ready.

Nearest point of departure:	Freeport
Winter/summer water temperature:	65°F/84°F
Typical depth range:	52–80 feet
Typical water conditions:	Highly variable
Visibility:	To 125 feet
Expertise required:	Intermediate

After an eight-hour boat ride, and perhaps months of anticipation, your first glimpse of these unique reefs may be deceptively disappointing. From just below the water surface they appear to be merely an ordinary rocky bottom. But after you descend 55 to 60 feet, the landscape turns into a wild array of spectacular coral heads measuring up to 10 feet across. Huge boulders of mountainous star coral and brain coral covered by brilliantly colored sponges jut upwards, providing an urban-like setting for more than 500 species of fish, macro-invertebrates, and algae.

The Flower Gardens, Texas' backyard Caribbean reefs, are located 110 miles southeast of Galveston. The large corals and colorful encrusting sponges make these two reefs the state's premier offshore diving destination.

The spectacular scenery afforded by 100-foot visibility at these marine gardens astonishes first-time divers.

A curious rock beauty peers out of a secure coral recess.

The East and West Flower Garden Banks lie atop salt domes 110 miles southeast of Galveston at the edge of the Texas-Louisiana outer continental shelf. Situated 12 miles apart in 400 feet of water, these reefs are the northernmost reef system on the North American continental shelf. The crest of the East Flower Garden Bank covers 400 acres and lies 52 feet from the surface. The West Flower Garden Bank grows up to 66 feet from the surface and covers 100 acres at the crest. Their very existence has intrigued marine scientists because they lie at the fringe of normal reef-building habitat, 500 miles from their closest coral neighbor near Tampico, Mexico.

For the thrill of a lifetime, watch for the magnificent Atlantic manta gliding in from the depths off the shelf. These gentle and curious crea-

The Spanish hogfish, a common inhabitant of the Flower Gardens, is most often seen in its juvenile form. It spends much of its time eating external parasites from other fish.

tures, which can span 20 feet across at the wingtips, seem to enjoy being touched or even ridden by divers. Even if the manta aren't there on the day you dive, there's enough excitement in watching reef denizens like the spiny lobster, feather worms, thorny oysters, grouper, amberjack, great barracuda, red snapper, and a host of tropical fish. Of special interest at

The queen angelfish is one of the most colorful tropical fish of these reef communities.

A smooth trunkfish and stoplight parrotfish investigate the bottom for food.

the West Flower Gardens, but not accessible by divers, is a small brine lake discovered at 220 feet in 1976 by Texas A&M University oceanographer Dr. Tom Bright, in the submersible *Diaphus.*

Sadly, you will also see the abandoned chains, overturned coral heads, and wide, deep gouges caused by anchoring. After a ten-year battle by marine scientists, divers and public officials, the Flower Gardens were finally designated in 1992 as a National Marine Sanctuary under the Marine Sanctuary Program established in 1972. The Marine and Estuary

Colonies of tiny coral polyps have lived and died at this site for 20,000 years, creating a delicate and complex ecosystem.

On a night dive at the Flower Gardens, one may encounter the colorful spiny lobster. ▼

The main attraction at the Flower Gardens is the Atlantic manta. Curious and gentle, these majestic creatures can be seen on most visits, and a lucky diver may be able to hitch a ride.

Graceful tentacles of the nocturnal tube anemone extend into the darkness to feed on passing zooplankton.

Visitors to the Flower Gardens are always astonished at the large brain corals and diverse fish life.

Management Division of the National Oceanographic and Atmospheric Administration (NOAA) authorized the designation. Regulation of oil and gas activities, anchoring, and vessel sizes will protect these reefs from additional damage.

Along the same lines, refrain from spearfishing in the Flower Gardens. Spears can become embedded in the live corals, further damaging the reefs. For additional information, contact your local dive shop.

The Department of Oceanography at Texas A&M University is involved in an intensive environmental monitoring study sponsored by the Department of the Interior's Minerals Management Service. You may see metal rods extending out of both live and dead coral heads. *Do not disturb these marker rods.* They are in place to measure long-term changes in coral growth and conditions. If these rods are tampered with in any way, a wealth of information may be lost.

Mobil H.I. 389   19

Nearest point of departure:	Freeport
Winter/summer water temperature:	65°F/85°F
Typical depth range:	Bottom at 400 feet; maximum safety dive 150 feet
Typical water conditions:	Variable
Visibility:	70–125 feet
Expertise required:	Intermediate

Located one mile from the West Bank of the Flower Garden Banks National Marine Sanctuary and within its protective boundaries, this fully operational platform is the focus of intense scientific study through the Flower Gardens Ocean Research Project (FGORP), an innovative, collab-

Mobil H.I. 389 is located within the Flower Garden's National Marine Sanctuary Boundary only one mile from the West Banks.

A diver photographs the sponge-encrusted legs of the platform. The underwater structure of 389 is notable for its unusual sponge development, with some of the tube sponges reaching lengths of 30 inches.

Cuban hogfish are common around the platform, but are seldom seen at the nearby Flower Garden Banks.

A large school of jack pass through the structure. Some jacks exceed four feet in length, and the schools often envelop divers.

orative venture between science and industry. Incredible sponge development highlights a highly productive, distinctly tropical, bluewater reef environment. Scientists believe it is the platform's proximity to the Flower Gardens, coupled with the influx of Caribbean currents, that contributes to making it one of the most unusual and spectacular artificial reef systems in the Gulf of Mexico. Curiously, the platform also provides habitat for marine life rarely found even in the Flower Gardens.

Covered with hydroids, sponges, and barnacles, the rig's jungle-gym crossbars and columns create an underwater cathedral visited by Cuban hogfish, French and Queen angelfish, blennies, and darting schools of amberjack, shark, and spadefish. Because of ongoing studies and the federal protection of this site, do not touch or take anything.

Many dive boats visiting the Flower Gardens make side excursions to this unusual platform. Check with dive shops offering tours to the Marine Sanctuary to confirm that Mobil H.I. 389 is on the itinerary. An opportunity to dive H.I. 389 shouldn't be missed!

Nearest point of departure:	Corpus Christi
Winter/summer water temperature:	55°F/82°F
Typical depth range:	30–45 feet
Typical water conditions:	Variable; currents can be very strong
Visibility:	15–25 feet (can change quickly)
Expertise required:	Intermediate

Named because it is located in about 46 feet (7½ fathoms) of water, this reef is situated 2 miles off Padre Island, 46 miles south of the northern entrance to the Padre Island National Seashore. Oriented in a NW-SE direction, the relief consists of a calcareous sandstone outcropping some 300 yards long and 60 yards wide. The area is probably the site of an ancient freshwater pond that existed during the twilight of the Pleistocene epoch. Within this time-frame, a vast, shallow sea (later known as the Gulf of Mexico) lay several miles to the south, due to a drop in ocean levels that

An Atlantic deer cowrie can grow to five inches and is a common inhabitant of offshore destinations.

Schools of snapper, jack, spadefish, and tomtate often appear from the murk and frequently follow divers across the reef.

occurred during the last ice age. The reef base may yet contain fossils of mammoth, camel, bison, and other animals that came there to drink.

Today, the dense, convoluted mound of rock is covered by a six- to ten-inch organic matrix composed of green algae, hydroids, bryozoans, ivory bush coral, and untold thousands of polycheate worm tubes. Within the depths of this lattice lie legions of tiny mollusks, crabs, pistol shrimp, and brittle stars. Delicate growths of colonial anemones drip from the margins of the reef like stalactites, mingling with clusters of tunicates, colorful sponges, and sea whips. Roving jack cravell, Atlantic spadefish, and black drum dart past in schools too quick to count, while red snapper and couch-sized jewfish lounge about in the trenches.

Neither spearfishing nor fish collecting from the reef is allowed. Divers must maintain neutral buoyancy and are asked to avoid touching the reef or its inhabitants. Seven and One-Half Fathom Reef has recently been nomi-

Tunicates and colorful sponges encrust most of the sandstone structure.

nated for inclusion in the GEMS (Gulf Ecological Management Site) program, a local, state, and national effort to coordinate research and conservation strategies for the benefit of natural resources in the Gulf of Mexico.

Call Copeland's Specialty Sports in Corpus Christi (512-854-1135) for more information about excursions to this reef (available from June through September, weather permitting).

4

Safety

This section discusses emergency procedures in case of a diving accident. We do not discuss the diagnosis or treatment of serious medical problems; refer to your first-aid manual, emergency diving accident manual, or qualified medical professional for that information.

DAN

The Divers Alert Network (DAN), a membership association of individuals and organizations sharing a common interest in diving safety, operates a 24-hour national hotline at 919-684-8111 (collect calls are accepted in a SCUBA emergency). DAN does not directly provide medical care. However, the network does provide medical advice on early treatment, evacuation, and hyperbaric treatment of diving-related injuries, as well as insurance to help cover the related costs. Additionally, DAN provides diving safety information to members to help prevent accidents. Membership is $25 per year for an individual and $35 per year for a family. Insurance costs are extra and range from $25 to $35. Other membership benefits include:

- The DAN Dive and Travel Medical Guide (DTMG), which describes symptoms of and first aid for the major diving-related injuries.
- A membership card listing DAN's emergency and nonemergency phone numbers for diving, a toll-free number for nondiving emergency medical evacuations, and the DAN TRAVEL/ASSIST number (202-296-9620 or 800-326-3822) which arranges all medical transportation and limited visitor transportation in an emergency situation.
- One tank decal and three small equipment decals with DAN's logo and emergency number.
- Oxygen first aid training program.
- A bi-monthly magazine, *Alert Diver,* which describes dive medicine and safety information in layman's language and contains case histories, articles for professionals, and medical questions related to diving.

Special sponsorship for dive stores, dive clubs, and corporations is also available. The DTMG manual can be purchased for $7 from the DAN Membership Services Department at 800-446-2671.

Dive equipment should always be checked prior to taking your trip.

DAN divides the U.S. into seven regions, each coordinated by a specialist in diving medicine who has access to the skilled hyperbaric chambers in his region. Non-emergency or information calls are connected to the DAN office and information number at 919-684-2948. This number can be dialed directly, Monday–Friday, between 9:00 a.m. and 5:00 p.m. Eastern Standard time. Chamber status can change frequently, making this kind of information dangerous if obsolete at the time of an emergency. Instead, divers should contact DAN as soon as a diving emergency is suspected. All divers should have comprehensive medical insurance and check to make sure that hyperbaric treatment and air ambulance services are covered internationally.

Diving is a safe sport, and there are very few accidents compared to the number of dives made each year and number of divers. But when the infrequent injury does occur, DAN is ready to help. DAN, originally 100% federally funded, is now largely supported by the diving public. Membership in DAN or purchase of DAN manuals or decals provides divers with useful safety information and provides DAN with necessary operating funds. Donations to DAN are tax deductible, as DAN is a legal non-profit public service organization.

Emergency Services

In any emergency, your simplest and quickest contact for help is to dial 911. The decision to obtain the services of a hyperbaric chamber for treatment of a diving injury should be made by a certified physician trained in dive medicine, or after consultation with DAN. Some hyperbaric facilities in Texas may not have experience in treating SCUBA injuries. They may not remain open for 24-hour treatment of diving injuries unless they have patients in-house. They may also lack 24-hour staffing by physicians trained in dive medicine. However, the following numbers may be able to provide additional information or assistance:

Offshore Rescue:

U.S. Coast Guard
(409) 766-5620
UHF Radio: Channel 16

Hospitals/Recompression Facilities

St. David's Community Hospital/Hyperbaric Unit
919 East 32nd Street
Austin, Texas 78705
24-hour phone: (512) 397-4145

St. Elizabeth Hospital Hyperbaric Center
2830 Calder
Beaumont, Texas 77702
24-hour phone: (409) 892-7171

Texas A&M Hyperbaric Center/Beutel Health Center
Texas A&M University
College Station, Texas 77843
24-hour phone: (409) 845-1511

Memorial Medical Center/Hyperbaric Unit
2606 Hospital Blvd.
Corpus Christi, Texas 78405
24-hour phone: (512) 881-4000

Hyperbaric Medicine Unit Presbyterian Hospital of Dallas Institute for Exercise and Environmental Medicine
7232 Greenville Avenue
Dallas, Texas 75231
24-hour phone: (214) 788-6185

Memorial City Medical Center/Hyperbaric Unit
920 Frostwood
Houston, Texas 77024
24-hour phone: (713) 932-3000

University of Texas Medical Branch
310 University Blvd., Route 1115
Galveston, Texas 77555-1115
24-hour phone: (409) 772-1307

McAllen Medical Center Attn. Hyperbaric Oxygen Unit
301 W. Expressway 83
McAllen, Texas 78503
24-hour phone: (210) 632-4000

Southwest Texas Methodist Hospital/Hyperbaric Unit
4499 Medical Drive, SL-2
San Antonio, Texas 78229
24-hour phone: (210) 615-8334

Diver Guidelines for Protecting Fragile Marine Habitats

1. Maintain proper buoyancy control and avoid over-weighting.
2. Use correct weight belt position to stay horizontal, i.e., raise the belt above your waist to elevate your feet/fins, and move it lower toward your hips to lower them.
3. Use your tank position in the backpack as a balance weight, i.e., raise your backpack on the tank to lower your legs, and lower the backpack on the tank to raise your legs.
4. Watch for buoyancy changes during a dive trip. During the first couple of days, you'll probably breathe a little harder and need a bit more weight than the last few days.
5. Be careful about buoyancy loss at depth; the deeper you go the more your wet suit compresses, and the more buoyancy you lose.
6. Photographers must be extra careful. Cameras and equipment affect buoyancy. Changing f-stops, framing a subject, and maintaining position for a photo often conspire to prohibit the ideal "no-touch" approach on a reef. So, when you must use "holdfasts," choose them intelligently.
7. Avoid full leg kicks when working close to the bottom and when leaving a photo scene. When you inadvertently kick something, stop kicking! Seems obvious, but some divers either semi-panic or are totally oblivious when they bump something.
8. When swimming in strong currents, be extra careful about leg kicks and handholds.
9. Attach dangling gauges, computer consoles, and octopus regulators. They are like miniature wrecking balls to a reef.
10. Never drop boat anchors onto a reef.

Appendix 1: Dive Shops

This information is included as a service to the reader. The authors have made every effort to make this list accurate at the time of printing. This list does not constitute an endorsement of these operators and dive shops. If operators/owners wish to be considered for future reprints/editions, please contact Pisces Books, P.O. Box 2608, Houston, Texas 77252-2608.

Coastal Texas

Will's Underwater
101 N. Main
Baytown, Texas 77520
(713) 428-1490

Aquaventures Dive Shop
4099-B Calder
Beaumont, Texas 77706
(409) 899-5331

Sea See Divers
4012 Weber
Corpus Christi, Texas 78411
(512) 853-3483

Copeland's Specialty Sports
4041 S. Padre Island Drive
Corpus Christi, Texas 78411
(512) 854-1135

**Diver's Education &
Equipment Place**
4104 Seawall Blvd.
Galveston, Texas 77550
(409) 765-9746

Treasure Cove Scuba
620 51st Street
Galveston, Texas 77551
(409) 762-8422

Island Sea Sports, Inc.
736 Tarpon Street
Port Aransas, Texas 78373
(512) 749-4167

American Diving
1807 Padre Blvd.
South Padre Island, Texas 78597
(210) 761-2030

Ocean Quest Dive Center
5009 Padre Blvd. #14
South Padre Island, Texas 78597
(210) 761-5003

Dolphin Divers
9501-B Navarro
Victoria, Texas 77904
(512) 576-6770

Discover Diving
3010 19th Street
Beaumont, Texas 77706
(409) 898-7828

East Texas

Athens Scuba Park
601 North Murchison
Athens, Texas 75751
(903) 675-5762

M & M Scuba Lake Jackson
716 N. Hwy. 288
Clute, Texas 77531
(409) 299-DIVE

Golden Mermaid
2420 North Frazier
Conroe, Texas 77301
(409) 539-3483

Divetech, Inc.
8713-A Katy Freeway
Houston, Texas 77024
(713) 973-2946

Houston Scuba Academy
12505 Hillcroft
Houston, Texas 77079
(713) 497-7651

Kenlee's Scuba West
5539 Richmond Ave.
Houston, Texas 77056
(713) 784-1173

Ocean Sports, Inc.
5245 Buffalo Speedway
Houston, Texas 77005
(713) 880-1287

Oceanic Ventures
2715 Bissonnet #302
Houston, Texas 77005
(713) 523-3483

Pro Scuba
9717 Westheimer
Houston, Texas 77042
(713) 783-3483

Sea Sports Scuba
10971 Northwest Freeway
Houston, Texas 77092
(713) 688-7777

W.W. Diving Co.
1307 1st Street
Humble, Texas 77338
(713) 540-1616

Scubasport
121 West Pipeline Road
Hurst, Texas 76053
(817) 282-4626

The Dive Shop
996 Cherry Creek Rd.
Dayton, Texas 77535
(409) 258-5241

Scubatec
307 North Timberland
Lufkin, Texas 75901
(817) 282-4626

Diver's Depot
720 South Street
Nacogdoches, Texas 75961
(409) 564-3483

Adventure Scuba Quest
17611 Kuykendahl
Spring, Texas 77379
(713) 320-0001

Scuba Center
3320 Troup Highway
Suite 130
Tyler, Texas 75701
(903) 595-2703

Discover Scuba
15106 Highway 3
Webster, Texas 77598
(713) 480-8530

Sport Divers of Houston, Inc.
125 West Bay Area Blvd.
Webster, Texas 77598-4111
(713) 338-1611

Central Texas

A.K.A. Divers
2150 North Collins
Arlington, Texas 76011
(817) 275-2181

Arlington Scuba Center
2414 West Park Row Drive
Arlington, Texas 76013
(817) 265-6712

Pisces Scuba
11401 RR 2222
Austin, Texas 78730
(512) 258-6646

Scubaland Adventures
9515 North Lamar
Suite 154
Austin, Texas 78753
(512) 339-0733

Tom's Dive & Ski, Inc.
5909 Burnet Road
Austin, Texas 78757
(512) 451-3425

Totally Scuba
603 North IH-35
Belton, Texas 76513
(817) 939-1458

Scuba Magic, Inc.
1235 South Josey Lane
Carrolton, Texas 75006
(214) 416-3644

For Divers Only
College Park Business Center
1015 East I-35 North
Suite 324
Carrolton, Texas 75006
(214) 446-3483

Sea-U Underwater
900 Harvey Road #5
College, Station, Texas 77840
(409) 693-1867

Aqua Adventures Greenville, Inc.
6846 Greenville, Ave.
Suite 100
Dallas, Texas 75231
(214) 696-6090

Dive West
4701 Frankford #213
Dallas, Texas 75287
(214) 248-8188

Sand & Sea Scuba
9410 Walnut Street
Suite 112
Dallas, Texas 75229
(214) 690-3483

The Scuba Shop
14440 Midway Road
Dallas, Texas 75244
(214) 404-8797

Island Divers Inc.
1731 West University Drive
Denton, Texas 76201
(817) 383-3483

Cuda Dive Shop
7410 Grapevine Highway
Suite E
Ft. Worth, Texas 76180
(817) 284-0451

Lone Star Scuba
2815 Altamere Drive
Ft. Worth, Texas 76116
(817) 377-3483

Scubasphere, Inc.
6703 Camp Bowie
Ft. Worth, Texas 76116
(817) 731-1461

Aqua World, Inc.
5418 Broadway Blvd.
Garland, Texas 75043
(214) 240-4559

Outdoor Adventures
1122 Highway 4 South
Granbury, Texas 76049
(817) 573-3426

Tucker's Dive Shop
2025 East Main Street
Grand Prairie, Texas 75050
(214) 264-7305

Adventures in Scuba
3225 West Airport Freeway
Suite 228
Irving, Texas 75062
(214) 594-7234

Scuba Plus
422 West Business Highway 190
Killeen, Texas 76541
(817) 773-4220

Divers Isle
902 N. Beckley
Lancaster, Texas 75146
(214) 230-1481

Dive West, Inc.
1108 Dobie Drive
Suite 103
Plano, Texas 75074
(214) 424-6563

Ocean's Window Scuba Center
2301 North Central Expressway
#140
Plano, Texas 75075
(214) 423-3483

Dive Masters of San Antonio, Inc.
5421 Grisson Road
San Antonio, Texas 78238
(210) 684-3483

Dive World
8507 North McCullough
San Antonio, Texas 78216
(512) 340-3721

Trident Diving Equipment
2110 West Avenue
San Antonio, Texas 78201
(512) 734-7442

Tropical Divers
12241 San Pedro Ave.
Suite 120
San Antonio, Texas 78216
(210) 490-3483

The Dive Shop
P.O. Box 2130
1911 Ranch Road #12
San Marcos, Texas 78667
(512) 396-3483

Scuba Plus: The Dive Shop
3402 South General Bruce Drive
Temple, Texas 76504
(817) 773-4220

Duggan Diving
928 Coronado Blvd.
Universal City, Texas 78148
(210) 658-7496

Sea-N-Ski
6001 West Waco Drive #614
Waco, Texas 76710
(817) 751-1773

West Texas

School of Scuba
942 Walnut Street
Abilene, Texas 79603
(915) 673-2949

Underwater Connection
2950 North 1st
Abilene, Texas 79603
(915) 677-0337

Diver's Pen
3701 Plains Blvd.
Ste. 112
Amarillo, Texas 79106
(806) 358-7895

Scuba Sportz
2618 Wolfin Village
Amarillo, Texas 79109
(806) 355-3443

Desert Scuba, Inc.
9509 Viscount
El Paso, Texas 79925
(915) 593-DIVE

Inner Space S.C.U.B.A.
4000 North Mesa
El Paso, Texas 79902
(915) 532-4107

Lynx Dive & Sports Inc.
213 Village Blvd.
Ste. 1-B
Laredo, Texas 78441
(210) 712-3483

The Best Little Dive Shop in Texas
4401 82nd Street
Unit 1500
Lubbock, Texas 79424
(806) 794-3483

Stovall's Scuba Center
3303 North Midkiff
Suite 115
Midland, Texas 79705
(915) 699-5959

Adventure Scuba
1215 East 8th Street
Odessa, Texas 79761
(915) 580-4545

Desert Oasis Dive Shop
PO Box 11
Toyahvale, Texas 79786
(915) 375-2572

Appendix 2: Equipment Checklist

Diving Equipment

—— tank
—— backpack
—— regulator
—— mask
—— fins
—— snorkel
—— wetsuit
—— boots
—— gloves
—— weight belt
—— pressure gauge
—— depth gauge

—— dive computer
—— B. C.
—— knife
—— compass
—— dive bag
—— dive light
—— batteries or charger
—— dive tables
—— log book
—— watch
—— bottom timer
—— dive flag

—— "glow sticks"
—— odds and ends kit
—— "O rings"
—— protective clothing
—— nylon line
—— flag and float
—— slate
—— buoy
—— lift bag
—— fishing license

Personal Items

—— shirts
—— shorts
—— underclothing
—— shoes
—— sandals
—— sunscreen
—— soap
—— deodorant

—— toothbrush
—— hair dryer
—— travel clock
—— pants
—— swimsuit
—— socks
—— hat
—— sunglasses

—— medications
—— shampoo
—— toothpaste
—— hairbrush
—— comb
—— scissors

Photo Equipment

—— camera bodies
—— tripod
—— light meter
—— strobe arm
—— chargers
—— ports

—— lens cleaner
—— extra parts
—— lenses
—— strobes
—— extension tubes
—— batteries

—— housings
—— film
—— tool kit
—— silicone grease

Appendix 3:
Maps of Parks/Campgrounds
Near Dive Sites*

Balmorhea State Recreation Area

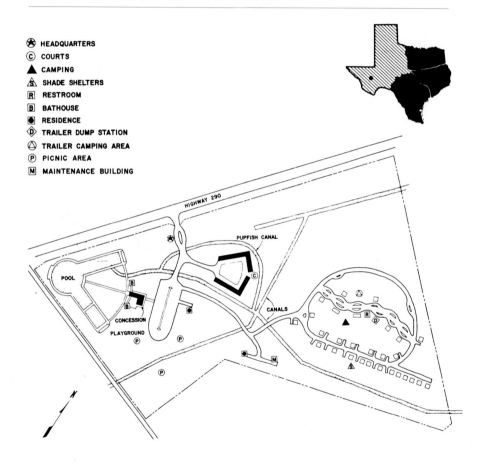

⊛ HEADQUARTERS
ⓒ COURTS
▲ CAMPING
⚠ SHADE SHELTERS
Ⓡ RESTROOM
Ⓑ BATHOUSE
◉ RESIDENCE
Ⓓ TRAILER DUMP STATION
△ TRAILER CAMPING AREA
Ⓟ PICNIC AREA
Ⓜ MAINTENANCE BUILDING

HIGHWAY 290
PUPFISH CANAL
POOL
CANALS
CONCESSION
PLAYGROUND
N

---

*From *Camper's Guide to Texas Parks, Lakes, and Forests,* 3rd Edition by
Mickey Little, Gulf Publishing Co., Houston, Texas © 1990.

Lake Amistad

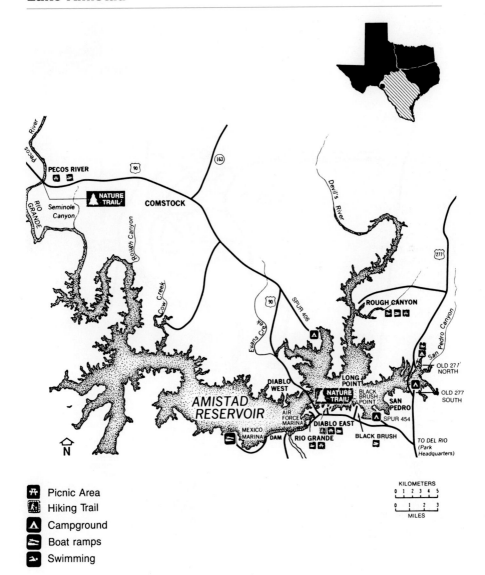

- 🛌 Picnic Area
- 🚶 Hiking Trail
- ⛺ Campground
- 🛥 Boat ramps
- 🏊 Swimming

Garner State Park (Frio River)

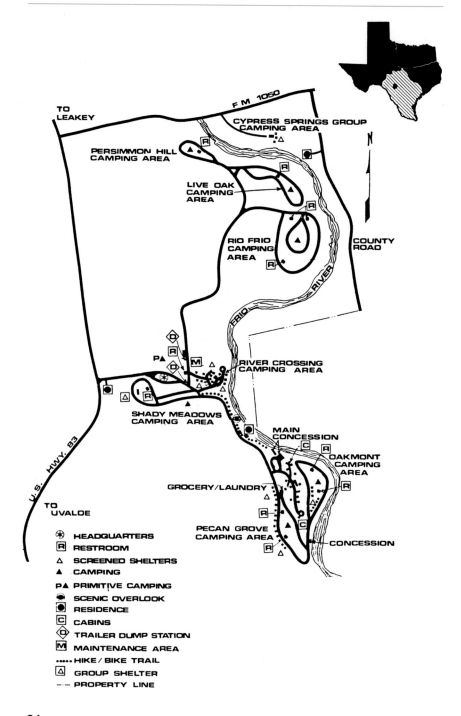

Canyon Lake

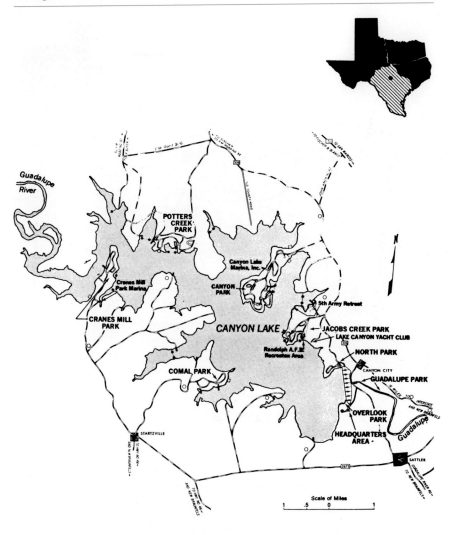

Lake Travis

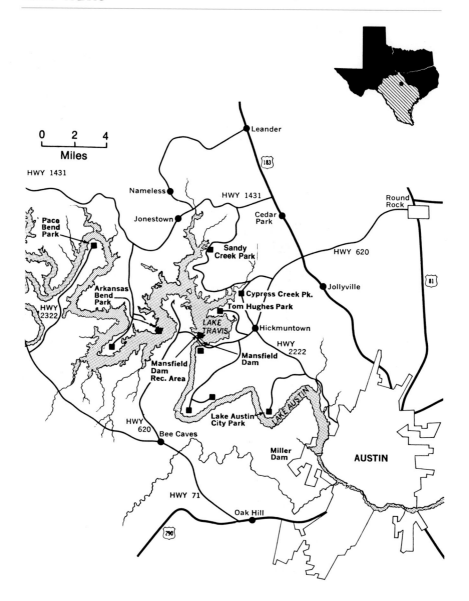

0   2   4
Miles

HWY 1431

Leander

183

Nameless

HWY 1431

Jonestown

Cedar
Park

Round
Rock

Pace
Bend
Park

Sandy
Creek Park

HWY 620

Arkansas
Bend
Park

Jollyville

81

HWY
2322

Cypress Creek Pk.

Tom Hughes Park

LAKE
TRAVIS

Hickmuntown

HWY
2222

Mansfield
Dam
Rec. Area

Mansfield
Dam

LAKE AUSTIN

HWY
620

Lake Austin
City Park

Bee Caves

Miller
Dam

AUSTIN

HWY 71

Oak Hill

290

Possum Kingdom State Recreation Area

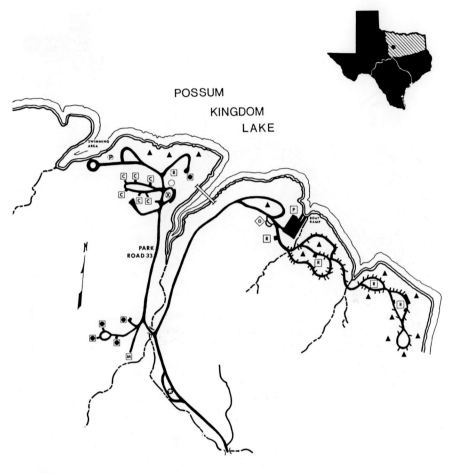

POSSUM

KINGDOM

LAKE

PARK
ROAD 33

N

LEGEND

- ✪ Headquarters
- ▣ Residence
- Ⓒ Cabin
- Ⓡ Restroom
- ⓧ Playground
- ○ Concession
- ◈ Trailer Dump Station
- Ⓟ Parking Area
- Ⓜ Maintenance
- ▲ Camping
- ⊨ Fishing Pier
- ₽ Picnicking

Huntsville State Park

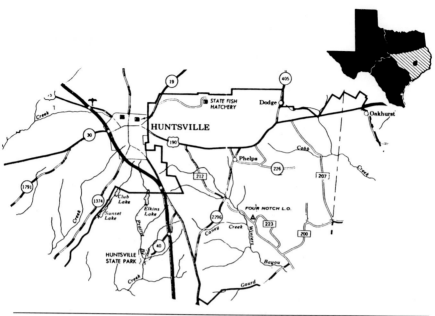

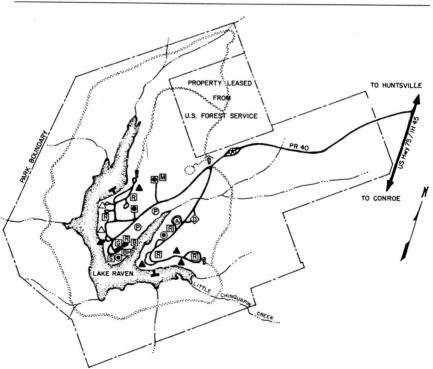

Toledo Bend Reservoir

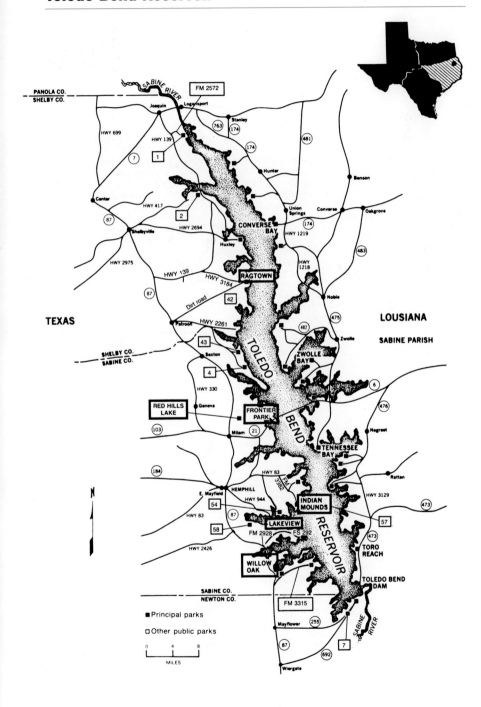

Index

 **Pisces Books®**

Be sure to check out these other great books from Pisces:

Caribbean Reef Ecology
Great Reefs of the World
Skin Diver Magazine's Book of Fishes, 2nd Edition
Shooting Underwater Video: A Complete Guide to the Equipment and Techniques for
    Shooting, Editing, and Post-Production
Snorkeling . . . Here's How, 2nd Ed.
Watching Fishes: Understanding Coral Reef Fish Behavior
Watersports Guide to Cancun

Diving and Snorkeling Guides to:

Australia: Coral Sea and Great Barrier Reef
Australia: Southeast Coast and Tasmania
The Bahamas: Family Islands and Grand
    Bahama
The Bahamas: Nassau and New Providence
    Island, 2nd Ed.
Bali
Belize
Bermuda
The Best Caribbean Diving
Bonaire
The British Virgin Islands
California's Central Coast
The Cayman Islands, 2nd Ed.
Cocos Island
Cozumel, 2nd Ed.
Cuba
Curacao
Fiji
Florida's East Coast, 2nd Ed.
The Florida Keys, 2nd Ed.

The Great Lakes
Guam and Yap
The Hawaiian Islands, 2nd Ed.
Jamaica
Northern California and the Monterey
    Peninsula, 2nd Ed.
The Pacific Northwest
Palau
Puerto Rico
The Red Sea
Roatan and Honduras' Bay Islands
St. Maarten, Saba, and St. Eustatius
Scotland
Seychelles
Southern California, 2nd Ed.
Texas
Truk Lagoon
The Turks and Caicos Islands
The U.S. Virgin Islands, 2nd Ed.
Vanuatu

Available from your favorite dive shop, bookstore, or directly from the publisher: Pisces Books®, a division of Gulf Publishing company, Book Division, Dept. AD, P.O. Box 2608, Houston, Texas 77252-2608. (713) 520-4444.

Include purchase price plus $4.95 for shipping and handling. IL, NJ, PA, and TX residents add appropriate tax.

We hope you have a lot of "up-front and personal" encounters with the underwater critters of Texas—like this parrotfish in "far east" Texas.